Have you ever seen a dragonfly sitting close by?

They come in so many shapes and sizes! Watch them as they fly.

Dragonflies have two antennae,
but they are very small.

Unless you look quite closely,
you might not see them at all!

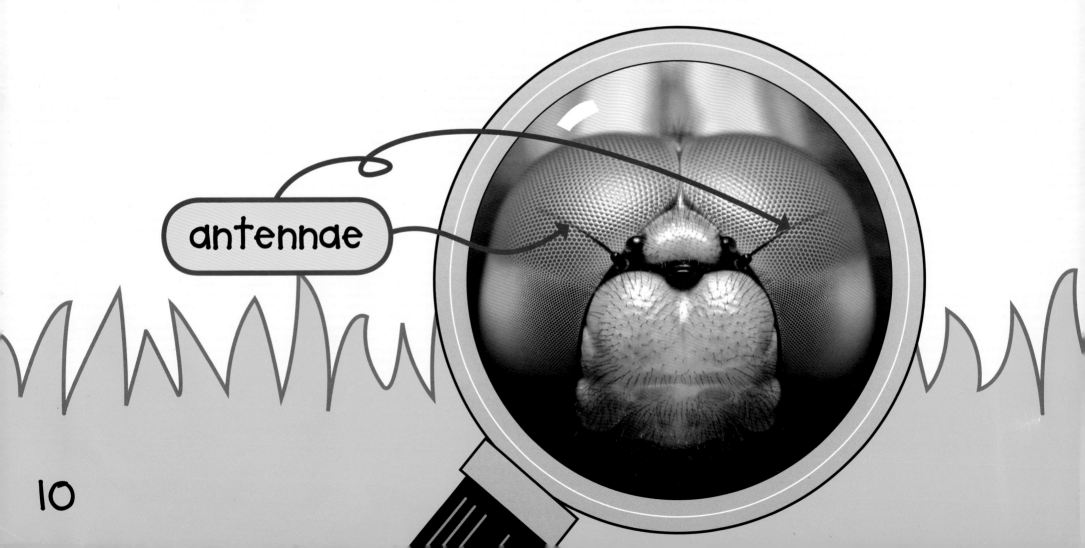

antennae

How many wings do you see on this dragonfly? 1, 2, 3, and 4.

Its four strong wings help the dragonfly to soar!

13

What colour are dragonflies?
Are they dull or are they bright?

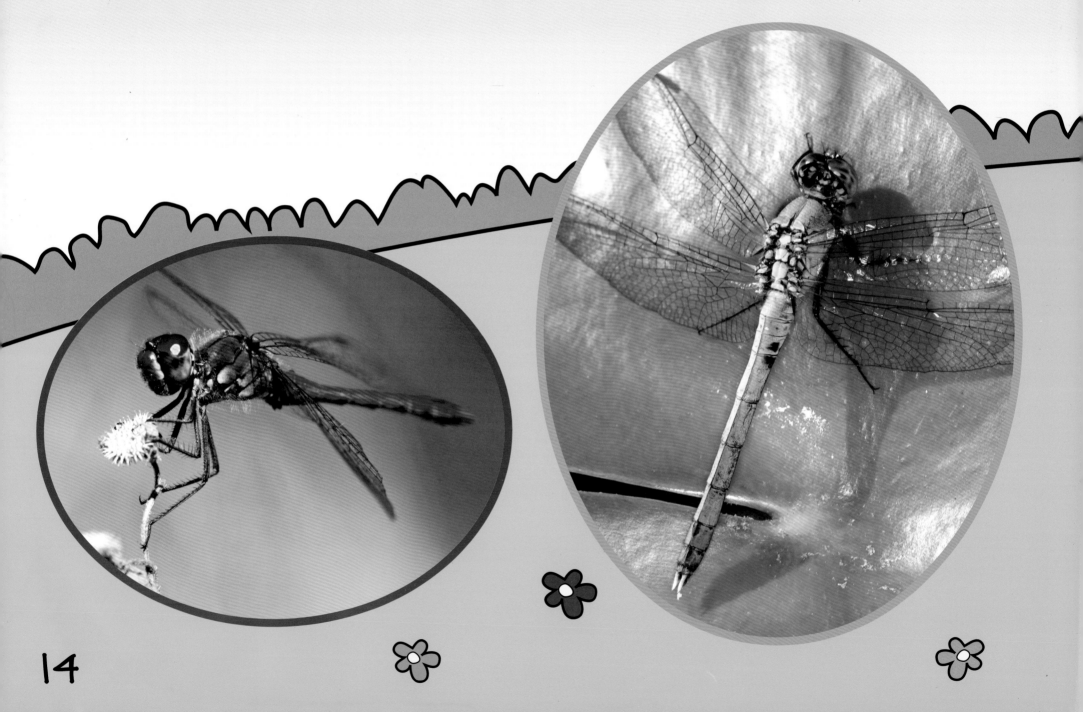

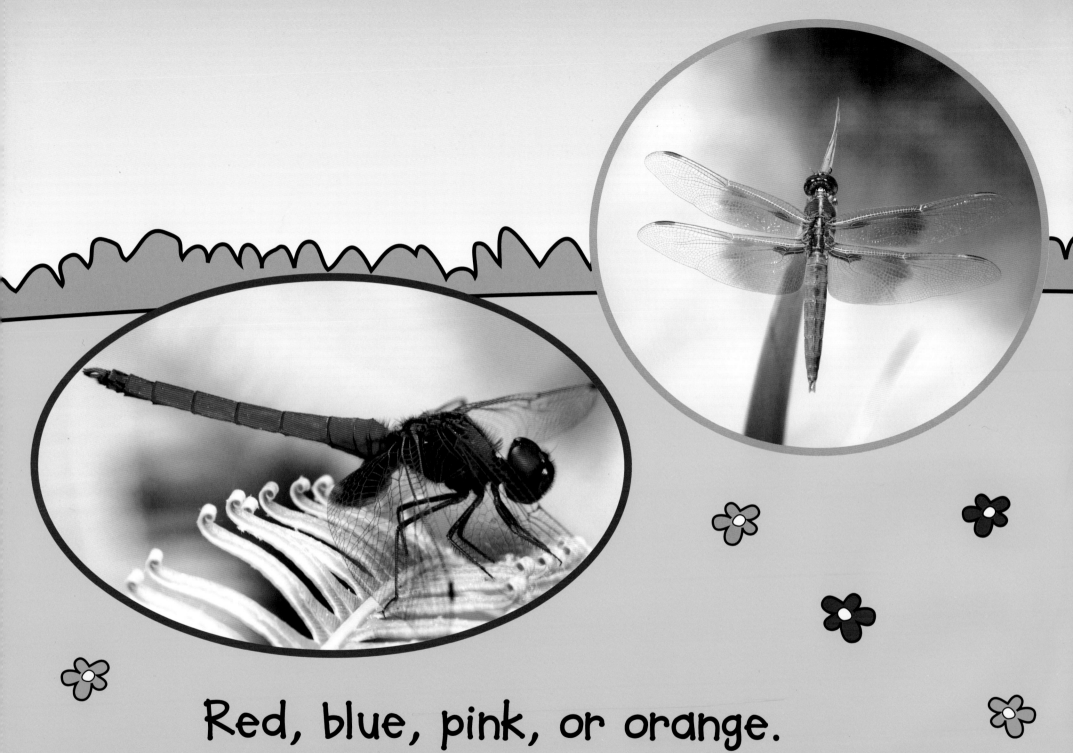

Red, blue, pink, or orange.
Dragonflies make a pretty sight!

Dragonflies don't just fly.
They also walk and climb.

Their six legs help them to
move around in record time!

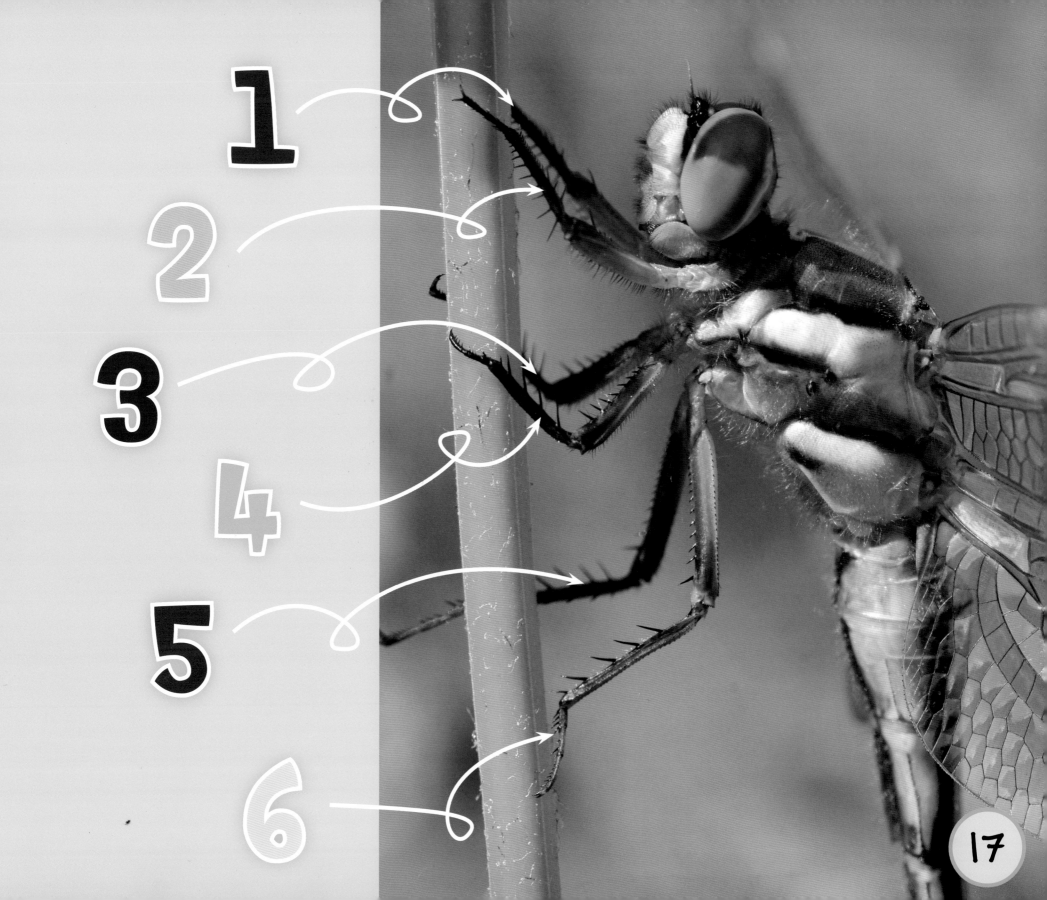

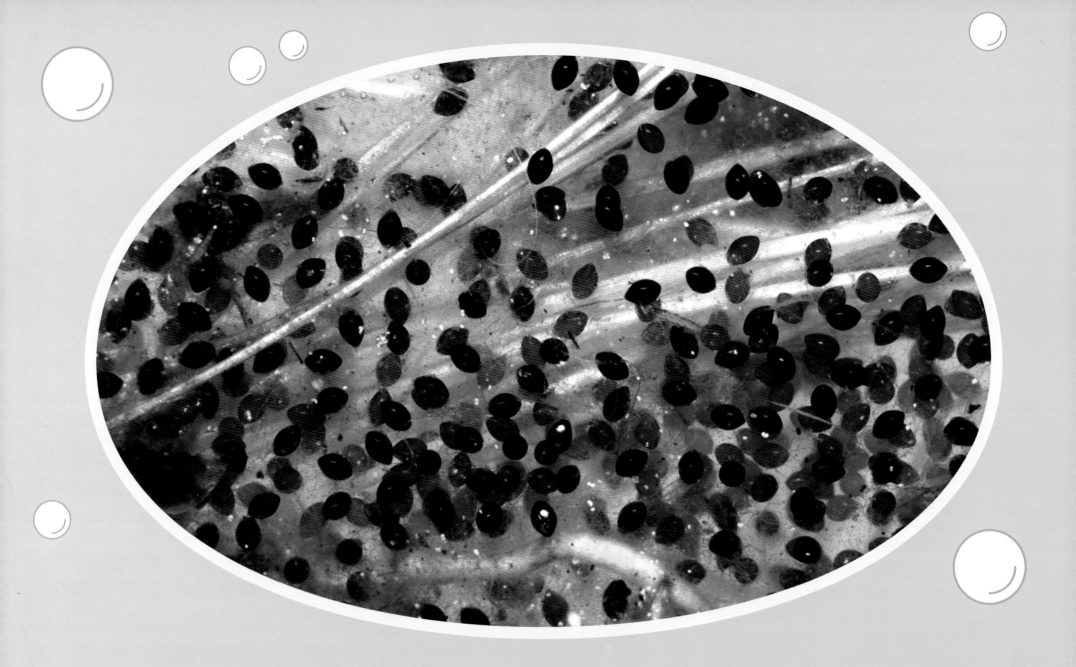

Dragonflies lay eggs in water,
which hatch into babies there.

These little nymphs soon become dragonflies that fly through the air!

nymph

Dragonflies like all water,
or that's the way it seems!

Look for dragonflies if you're near
big puddles, lakes, or streams!

21

Counting dragonflies

How many dragonflies can you count?
Some are brown and some are blue.

Look for dragonflies all around,
and you could find quite a few!

Did you know?

Dragonflies can fly backwards.

Index